EXPLORE SPACE!

EXPLORE THE STARS

BY EMMA HUDDLESTON

CONTENT CONSULTANT
MARCEL AGÜEROS, PhD
ASSOCIATE PROFESSOR OF ASTRONOMY
COLUMBIA UNIVERSITY

Kids Core
An Imprint of Abdo Publishing
abdobooks.com

abdobooks.com

Published by Abdo Publishing, a division of ABDO, PO Box 398166, Minneapolis, Minnesota 55439. Copyright © 2022 by Abdo Consulting Group, Inc. International copyrights reserved in all countries. No part of this book may be reproduced in any form without written permission from the publisher. Kids Core™ is a trademark and logo of Abdo Publishing.

Printed in the United States of America, North Mankato, Minnesota
052021
092021

Cover Photo: ESA/Goddard/NASA
Interior Photos: iStockphoto, 4–5; JPL-Caltech/NASA, 6, 13; ESA/Hubble/Goddard/NASA, 8; ESA/M. Livio and the Hubble 20th Anniversary Team (STScI)/NASA, 10–11; SDO/Goddard/NASA, 14; Hubble Heritage Team/Goddard/NASA, 17; CXC/CIERA/R. Margutti et al/SDSS/NASA, 18; Adam Pass Photography/Science Source, 20–21; Goddard/NASA, 22; Christian Darkin/Science Source, 23; Gerard Lodriguss/Science Source, 25; John Davis/Stocktrek Images/Science Source, 26; Shutterstock Images, 28–29

Editor: Marie Pearson
Series Designer: Katharine Hale

Library of Congress Control Number: 2020948336

Publisher's Cataloging-in-Publication Data

Names: Huddleston, Emma, author.
Title: Explore the stars / by Emma Huddleston
Description: Minneapolis, Minnesota : Abdo Publishing, 2022 | Series: Explore space! | Includes online resources and index.
Identifiers: ISBN 9781532195402 (lib. bdg.) | ISBN 9781644945445 (pbk.) | ISBN 9781098215712 (ebook)
Subjects: LCSH: Outer space--Exploration--Juvenile literature. | Stars--Juvenile literature. | Solar system--Juvenile literature. | Astronomy--Juvenile literature.
Classification: DDC 523.8--dc23

CONTENTS

The Sun provides Earth with daylight.

SCATTERED IN THE SKY

At nighttime, stars fill the sky. Some look brighter than others, depending on how close they are. The closest star to Earth is the Sun. It is also the brightest star in our sky. Unlike other stars in the sky, the Sun brings us daylight and warmth.

There are many stars at the center of the Milky Way galaxy.

Stars are huge bodies of hot gas. They are mostly made of hydrogen and helium gases. They can be different sizes. Dwarfs are small- or medium-sized stars. Our Sun is a dwarf star. Its **mass** is equal to about 333,000 Earths. Giant stars are larger, and supergiants are the biggest. Supergiants have a mass at least ten times greater than the Sun's.

Near and Far

A star's strong **gravity** keeps smaller objects in orbit around it. Orbiting is following a round path around another object. Earth is one of eight planets that orbit the Sun. Together, the Sun and its planets make up the solar system. The Sun orbits the center of the Milky Way galaxy. A galaxy is made up of many solar systems. There are about 300 billion stars in the Milky Way.

Seeing the Milky Way

On a cloudless night, ancient people could see the Milky Way anywhere in the world. It looked like a streak of bluish purple with bright dots. Today, humans make a lot of light at night. This makes it harder to see the Milky Way.

Scientists do not know how many stars are in the universe.

Besides the Sun, the rest of the stars in the sky are light-years away. A light-year is a measure of distance. It is how far a beam of light travels in one Earth year. One light-year equals about 5.9 trillion miles (9.5 trillion km).

Near and far, stars continue to amaze people. Scientists continue learning about stars in the Milky Way and beyond.

Explore Online

Visit the website below. Does it give any new information about light-years that wasn't in Chapter One?

What Is a Light-Year?

abdocorelibrary.com/explore-the
-stars

Stars form in nebulas such as the Carina Nebula.

CHAPTER 2

LIVING BILLIONS OF YEARS

Stars form in clouds of gas and dust called nebulas. Gravity pulls clumps of gas and dust together over millions of years. The growing clump gains mass. It becomes a protostar.

The protostar spins faster. Its central pressure and temperature increase. It will be a protostar for tens of thousands of years.

Eventually, the protostar core, or center, gets even hotter. Nuclear fusion begins. Nuclear fusion is when **nuclei** fuse, or join together. Hydrogen nuclei in the core fuse to make helium. This releases energy.

Burning Bright

When hydrogen fusion begins, the protostar becomes a main sequence star. Stars spend 90 percent of their lives in this stage. The Sun has been a main sequence star for more than 4.5 billion years. Scientists think it will spend another 5 billion years or more in this stage.

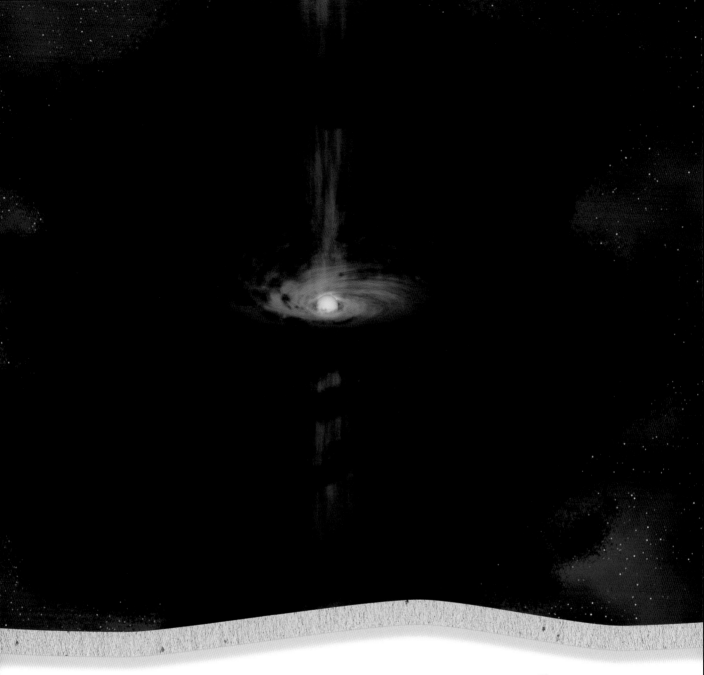

An illustration shows a protostar growing as it pulls in gas and dust from a surrounding nebula.

The lifetime of a star depends on its mass.

Smaller, less-massive stars have longer lifetimes.

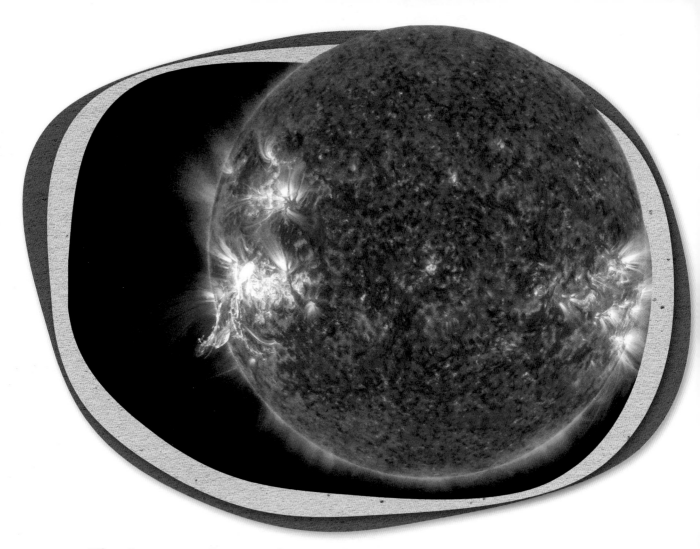

The hot gas that makes up the Sun and other main sequence stars sometimes shoots out from the surface.

Their main sequence stage may last trillions of years. Huge, massive stars burn through their hydrogen fuel faster. They may go through this stage in as few as 2 million years.

Stars about the size of the Sun become red giants when they cannot fuse any more hydrogen into helium. Then gravity makes a star's core **collapse**. This raises the core temperature. The hotter core causes outer layers to expand. They spread far apart and cool down. This makes the star look red. It is called a red giant.

When the Sun Swells

The Sun is in the main sequence stage. When it is a red giant, it will swell. Scientists think it may grow so large that it will swallow up the planets Mercury, Venus, and Earth.

Massive stars follow a similar path. They become red supergiants. Red supergiants are some of the most massive stars in the universe. A star spends much less of its lifetime as a red giant or supergiant than it does as a main sequence star. The Sun will be a red giant for only 1 billion years.

End of Life

At the end of the red giant stage, smaller stars fade. The outer layers of gas and dust are shed and form a planetary nebula. This leaves only the star's core. It is very **dense** and hot. It is called a white dwarf. White dwarfs can cool for billions of years. Then they become

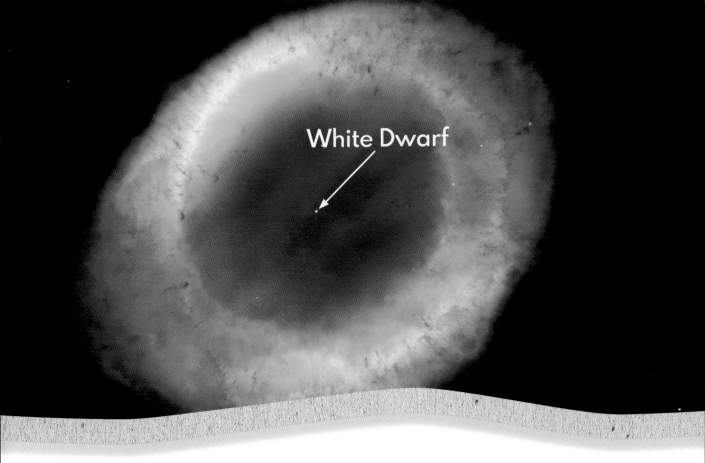

White Dwarf

A white dwarf is visible in the center of the planetary nebula known as the Ring Nebula.

black dwarfs. Black dwarfs are so cool they no longer glow.

Massive stars explode at the end of the red supergiant stage. The explosion is called a supernova. Supernovas shine for weeks. The outer layers get blasted into space.

Scientists captured this image of a supernova in January 2014.

The explosions create heavy **elements** such as iron. Elements help form other objects such as planets. They also help form living things.

After the explosion, the star will become one of two things. It may end life as a neutron star. This is the remaining core. It is smaller and denser than a white dwarf. It can spin thousands of times a second. Or the star will end life as a black hole. Black holes happen to stars ten times the size of the Sun or larger. The core is overwhelmed by gravity and collapses. It becomes a gravity pit. Anything that falls into a black hole cannot escape, including light. Scientists can't see black holes directly. They can study black holes by watching nearby matter fall in. When this happens, black holes can shoot out bright jets of **radiation**.

Further Evidence

Look at the website below. Does it give any new evidence about the Sun to support Chapter Two?

The Sun

abdocorelibrary.com/explore-the -stars

Stars look brighter in places
far from city lights.

CHAPTER 3

LOOKING AT STARS

Stars look like tiny dots in the sky. They may be different colors. And some are brighter than others. A star's true brightness is called luminosity. As stars go through life stages, their luminosity may change.

Special tools help scientists measure a star's luminosity.

Measuring a star's brightness is difficult from Earth. A faint star that is near Earth may look very bright. A bright star that is far away

Star Colors

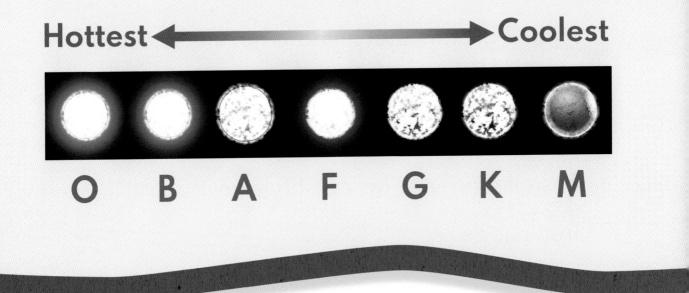

Hottest ⟵⟶ Coolest

O B A F G K M

Stars can be grouped by temperature into seven categories. Each category has a letter name. The hottest, O stars, look blue. The coolest, M stars, look red.

may look dull. So scientists use technology. Sensors can measure luminosity better than the human eye.

A star's color depends on its temperature. White and blue stars are the hottest. Cooler stars are orange or red.

Constellations

A group of stars that humans have connected in a certain shape is a constellation. There are more than 80 common constellations. Often, constellations are named after animals or Greek gods.

The North Star is always visible in the Northern Hemisphere. People have long used it to know the direction in which they are traveling. The star is part of the Ursa Minor constellation.

Not Just Stars

The night sky twinkles with dots of light. But not all bright objects in the sky are stars. Some are planets. Others are galaxies.

North Star

Ursa Minor means "Lesser Bear" in Latin. Polaris, or the North Star, is a part of this constellation.

That constellation is the same pattern that makes the Little Dipper. It is named for its shape, which is a sort of spoon.

Scientists can study the stars with special tools such as telescopes kept in observatories.

Since ancient times, people have used patterns of stars to find a direction or determine farming seasons. Today, scientists use constellations to identify where new stars are located. They are still learning more about stars!

Christian Sasse photographed the Milky Way in Australia. Sasse explained the images he took:

> What appeared were circular patterns with [natural] beauty. Each feature of the Milky Way has its own distinct pattern. . . . The Milky Way is creating this incredible pattern all the time.

Source: Nadia Drake. "See the Awesome March of the Milky Way across the Night Sky." *National Geographic*, 12 May 2017, nationalgeographic.com. Accessed 30 July 2020.

What's the Big Idea?

Read this quote carefully. What is its main idea? Explain how the main idea is supported by details.

SPACE NOTES

Star Life Cycle

Nebula

Protostar

Dwarf Main Sequence Star

Giant Main Sequence Star

Red Giant

Planetary
Nebula

White Dwarf

Black Dwarf

Neutron Star

Red Supergiant

Supernova

Black
Hole

Glossary

collapse
to cave in on oneself

dense
tightly packed together

elements
naturally occurring gases, solids, and liquids

gravity
a force that pulls objects toward each other

mass
a measurement of the amount of matter that makes up an object

nuclei
the centers of atoms, which are the building blocks of all matter; matter is any material that takes up space

radiation
the energy that something gives off

Online Resources

To learn more about stars, visit our free resource websites below.

Visit **abdocorelibrary.com** or scan this QR code for free Common Core resources for teachers and students, including vetted activities, multimedia, and booklinks, for deeper subject comprehension.

Visit **abdobooklinks.com** or scan this QR code for free additional online weblinks for further learning. These links are routinely monitored and updated to provide the most current information available.

Learn More

Kukla, Lauren. *Stars*. Abdo Publishing, 2017.

Nandi, Ishani, ed. *First Space Encyclopedia*. DK, 2016.

Star Finder! A Step-by-Step Guide to the Night Sky. DK, 2017.

Index

About the Author

Emma Huddleston lives in Minnesota with her husband. She enjoys writing books for young readers and staying active. She thinks learning about space is fascinating!